Christmas Bells

With warm friendly thoughts.

Fondly,

Cynthia Holt Cummings

Christmas Bells

Teddy bear story in verse by
Cynthia Holt Cummings
Illustrated by
Fritz Henning

Holt Peterson Press
Birmingham, Michigan

Christmas Bells

Teddy bear story in verse by
Cynthia Holt Cummings.
Illustrated by Fritz Henning

Copyright © 1995 by Holt Peterson Press, Inc.
*All rights reserved. No part of this book may be used or
reproduced in any manner whatsoever without written
permission from the publisher.*

Holt Peterson Press, Inc., Box 940
Birmingham, Michigan 48012

*Printed in the United States of America
First printing, June 1995.*

ISBN 1-881811-10-7

Cynthia gratefully dedicates
Christmas Bells to artist
Fritz, Jane and their family.

When Babette came to live
With the family of bears
She stood at the foot
Of the circular stairs,
In a gown of pink taffeta
Trimmed with lace
And a bonnet that almost
Covered her face,
She bowed and she curtsied
In her own little way
And the bears were so happy
When she decided to stay.

Babette opened the door
And then I saw
The smallest bear
With the tiniest paw,

She said "Come In
I'm serving Tea,
It will all be ready
At half past three".

There on the table
In pretty display,
Were the dainty cakes
She had baked that day.

11

Frosted in pink
And chocolate too
Lemon yellow
Green and blue,
All of the colors
To brighten a day,
Were there on the table
In pretty display.

There in the hall
By the circular stairs
Were gathered together
The family of bears.

Laughing and talking
While they waited for tea,
All were wondering
What the plan would be,
To bring joy to others
On Christmas Day,
They were anxious to hear
What Babette had to say.

Babette had seen
The big gray sleigh,
That was in the barn
Hidden away.

She became excited
At what she saw,
And gently touched it
With her tiny paw.

Layers of dust
Had collected there,
But it didn't discourage
This smallest bear.

She would ask Surprise
And Gusto too,
To make this sleigh
Look like new.

She could hardly wait
To be able to share,
Her plan for Christmas
With every bear.

Suddenly there was silence
The bears could hardly believe,
Babette was ready to tell them
The plan for Christmas Eve.

22

She told them
Of the big gray sleigh,
She had found in the barn
Hidden away.

She asked for their help
To make it like new,
There would be lots of work
Before they were through.

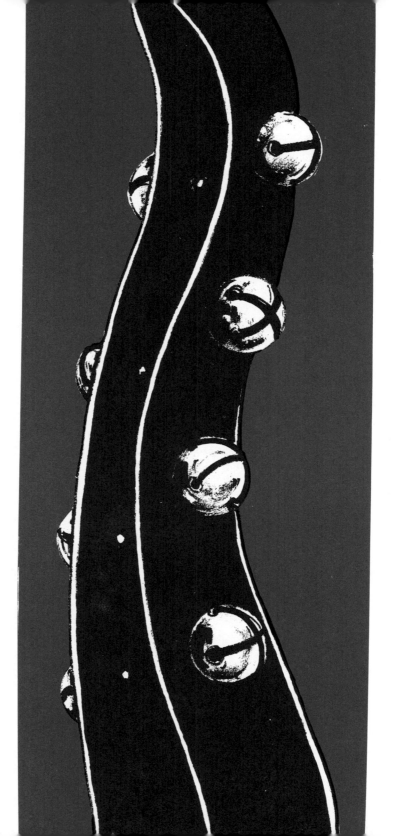

Then she would buy the silver bells
To be carried in the sleigh,
The Christmas surprise for the family of bears
Would be to give the bells away,
To all who came to the village square
To remember this Holy Night,
Standing beside the big fir tree
With its glow of Christmas light.

Surprise and Gusto
Worked each day,
Cleaning and painting
That big gray sleigh.

A color of red
That was ever so bright,
It was hard to keep hidden
And out of sight.
But the barn held their secret
And all they could see,
Was this beautiful sleigh
Near the big fir tree,
Filled with the bells
To be given away,
To all in the town
For Christmas Day.

During the Summer
When Babette went to shop,
She would reach the square
And always stop,

To look at the tree
That had grown so tall,
It made her feel
So very small,

But she pictured a star
At the top of the tree,
And the glow of light
That the town would see.

The blinking lights
On the branches below,
Would spread Christmas spirit
In the Winter snow.

There on the ground
Would be the red sleigh,
Filled with silver bells
To be given away.

They were raking leaves
And suddenly saw,
The smallest bear
With the tiniest paw.

She was really hurrying
Down the street,
They wondered
Where she was going,
Whom she would meet.

She waved her paw
In a friendly greeting,
But never a word
Of whom she was meeting.

Autumn was passing
Quickly by,
There were hints of Winter,
Dark clouds in the sky.

Carlisle, the shop owner
Waited for Babette,
And as the weeks passed
He would never forget,

To order the bells
When the salesman stopped by,
Carlisle never inquired
Or wondered why,

Babette bought the bells
On each shopping day,
And after her purchase
Would hurry away.

Patchwork and Mandy
Worked side by side,
Cutting red ribbons
In strips to be tied,

On each silver bell
To be given away,
With a teddy bear's love
For Christmas Day.

The little reindeer
Could hardly believe,
When he saw
What was happening Christmas Eve.

As he stood in the shadows
He suddenly saw,
The smallest bear
With the tiniest paw.

His little heart was beating fast
He hardly moved at all,
For he had never seen before
A bear that could be so small.

Her coat of red velvet
Touched the ground,
And the crunch of snow
Was the only sound,

As she hurried along
To the village square,
And her Christmas surprise
That would soon be there.

What a delight
What a surprise,
To see this bear
Of the smallest size.

The family of bears
Were on their way,
Pulling together
The big red sleigh.

Not a word was spoken
They could hardly wait,
To get to the square
Before too late.

It was a cold, cold night
Stars filled the sky,
There were lights in the houses
As they passed by.

Soon all of the people
Would come to the square,
And the teddy bear's surprise
Would be waiting there.

The bears would watch
As Babette gave away,
The silver bells
In the big red sleigh.

The little reindeer climbed
Into the sleigh,
And helped Babette
Give the bells away.

This was a Christmas
He would never forget,

How lucky he was
To have met Babette.

His little head
Turned to and fro
The bells were going fast;
Deep down
He really wished
This moment could always last.

Angel bear looked up from below
At the tree and the star
With its Christmas glow,
And she whispered the words
Once again, "Peace on Earth-
Good will towards men".

The teddy bear choir began to sing
Their voices came loud and clear,
Wishing all a Merry Christmas
With blessings in the coming year.

The sleigh remained
In the village square,
And the town
Would remember the day,
When a tiny reindeer
Helped Babette
Give the silver bells away.

The years went quickly by
But the town
Would never forget,
The smallest bear
With the tiniest paw
The family of bears' Babette.

And once again
The bells would ring,

With a Christmas
They had known,
In remembering.

The Author

Cynthia Holt Cummings, born in West Boylston, Massachusetts, graduated from Massachusetts General Hospital School for Nurses. During WWII, she served in the Army Nurse Corps with that hospital's reactivated unit . . . 6th General . . . from May 1942 through February 1946 including 33 months in North Africa and Italy.

Since 1948 she has lived in the Birmingham, Michigan area as a homemaker with her husband Dick, now retired. Their son, Roger, named after her youngest brother an Air Force gunner killed during WWII, is married to Buff and lives nearby with their four children . . . David, Julie, Jessica and Amanda.

In 1979 Cynthia's Christmas poetry written over the years for family and friends was consolidated and printed as that year's holiday greeting card. Accepting her husband's challenge, eight other books of new Christmas poetry, including three teddy bear stories, have since been published.

The Artist

The son of a noted illustrator, Fritz Henning grew up in the environs of an art studio and upon graduation from New York Maritime College, served as a ship's officer for a number of years before becoming a professional artist.

Long associated with the North Light Publications and with the Famous Artists School, Henning has been constantly involved in the world of visual art, including illustration, painting, designing, teaching and writing about the way of art and artists.

Recently retired to New Hampton, New Hampshire, Henning and his wife Jane have four children and 13 grandchildren.

Other illustrated books of Christmas poetry and verse by Cynthia Holt Cummings initially published in the indicated year by Holt Peterson Press, Inc., Box 940, Birmingham, Michigan 48012. Author narration on audio cassettes also available.

Teddy bear stories in verse:

Christmas Suprise, 1985
Christmas Joy, 1986
Christmas Spirit, 1989

Collections of short poems:

Christmas Ribbons, 1980
Christmas Memories, 1982
Christmas Love, 1984
Christmas Wishes, 1987
Christmas Treasures, 1988

Deluxe edition of previously published short Christmas poems with full color illustration by Fritz Henning:

Christmas Dreams, 1992